SHIPWRECK

Text by John Fowles
Photography by the Gibsons of Scilly

Jonathan Cape Thirty Bedford Square London

First published 1974
© 1974 by Jonathan Cape Ltd
Text © 1974 by Earth Resources
Research Ltd (KENNETH ALLSOP
MEMORIAL TRUST)

Jonathan Cape Ltd, 30 Bedford
Square, London WC1

ISBN 0 224 01053 0

Text set by
Cox & Wyman Ltd, London,
Fakenham and Reading

Printed in Great Britain by
The Westerham Press

Introduction

One day last February I stood with Rex Cowan, two divers and a boatman in one of the most splendid seascapes in Britain – among the reefs west of Annet in the Isles of Scilly. It was a fine day, very little swell; just enough to give white water on the black-serried granite fangs that stretched away in all directions. A few miles west rose the brave toy pinnacle of the loneliest of all lighthouses, the Bishop's Rock; razorbills dived, gannets glided majestically overhead, all around us amiable brown faces watched from the water ... and one young seal, a friend of the divers, yawned exactly like some dog impatient for a game. Difficult to imagine a place less tainted or more pleasurable on such a day; yet we floated in the very heart of what may well be the most terrible ten square miles in maritime history. It was not only that we were anchored even then over a wreck – the *Hollandia* of 1743, with its cargo of silver pieces of eight and ducatons. We could have anchored anywhere else in that area, and still have been over a wreck; in some places, layers of wrecks.

Rex the well-named began to point. Every rock, every islet, every reef had its long roll of sinister honour. That lazy lash of white over a black speck was the Retarrier, where the German liner *Schiller* struck one dreadful night in 1875 and 335 men and women drowned; and there the Crebinicks, the Crims, the Gunners, the Crebawethans; Rosevean and Rosevear, where down the centuries hundreds of sailors have wished they were drowned rather than marooned; the ill-named Jolly, Jacky's Rock, Gorregan, the Gilstone, which claimed the *Association* in 1707, heralding the worst disaster the Royal Navy has ever suffered out of action – 2,000 officers and men drowned in one night ... it was like a great gathering of murderers. Rex talked so fast I couldn't catch all the names. Only the same monotonous verb: struck, struck, struck. Our boatman and the divers knew these waters better than most of us know the streets of our home-town, yet they had to join in as well, point to more reefs, add more calamities. The past agony of some places drowns all present, and for evermore.

Proportionate to their size, no islands in the world have a more lethal record than the Scillies; and few mainland coasts can, in this dark rivalry, surpass those of West Cornwall. In the case

Schiller

Struck on the Retarrier Ledges near the Bishop's Rock lighthouse, May 7th, 1875. The Scottish-built *Schiller*, a crack large steamer of its time, was out of New York and calling at Plymouth *en route* for Hamburg. Owing to dense fog and the unfortunate habit of firing 'report' guns (to announce a safe crossing), the *Schiller*'s distress signals were ignored to begin with. The captain had to fire his revolver over the heads of the panicking passengers; then only two of the ship's eight boats were launched successfully. She began to break up fast in the heavy swell, and of the 372 passengers and crew, 335 drowned. The two lifeboats eventually came in at Tresco. The photograph shows one of them on the beach at St Mary's.

of the Scillies, the game was for long cruelly fixed against mariners. Before 1750 almost all charts, lazily copying ancient error, showed the islands ten miles north of their true position. The second black joke of the sea was not fully appreciated until very recently. An oceanic drift, the Rennell Current, sets round the Bay of Biscay and runs across the mouth of the English Channel. It is a knot an hour at most, but that is quite enough to push ships north of their supposed course. The Rennell, and not a wrong course by chart, almost certainly landed the *Schiller* on the Retarrier Ledges in 1875. All shipping to and from North Europe had and has to cope with the Scillies, and they have been nothing if not international in the toll they have taken through the centuries. A perennial problem with incoming vessels in the days of dead reckoning (establishing position by log and course steered, and not by sextant) was the need to make a recognizable landfall and know which of the two great channels, the Bristol or the English, one was in. An entire East Indies fleet in 1703 expected one morning to see themselves off Portsmouth; what rose out of their dawn was Lundy. In 1758 the captain of the French man-of-war *Belliqueux*, sailing from Canada to Brest, had exactly the same unwelcome sight when he came on deck – and paid for his bad navigation, since the Royal Navy pounced like a cat on this foolish mouse. The *Association* fleet was forty miles north of its supposed position, established by a conference of sailing masters four hours previously, when it struck. Defoe put the situation precisely in his *Tour*: 'These islands lye so in the middle between the two vast openings that it cannot, or perhaps never will be avoided' … as the *Torrey Canyon* was to discover in 1967.

The frequency of disaster, the remoteness, the atrocious economic disregard the rest of England always had for the Cornish and the Scillonians, gave rise to the very ancient occupation of wrecking. Properly the word has two meanings: wreck-inducing and wreck-plundering. The vast majority of the stories to do with the first activity – the false lights ('horn beacons' were lamps attached to a wandering clifftop cow), the true beacons that suffered a mysterious fuel crisis when they were most needed – are poorly attested or were distorted out of all proportion by the early advocates (well-to-do gentlemen, then as now) of law and order. Hawker of Morwenstow enshrined some of the names in verse and story: Cruel Coppinger, the Killigrews, Mawgan of Melhuach, Featherstone. He wrote one of his best curses on the last.

> Twist thou and twine! in light and gloom
>   A spell is on thine hand;
> The wind shall be thy changeful loom,
>   Thy web the shifting sand.

Twine from this hour, in ceaseless toil,
   On Blackrock's sullen shore;
Till cordage of the sand shall coil
   Where crested surges roar.

'Tis for that hour, when, from the wave,
   Near voices wildly cried;
When thy stern hand no succour gave,
   The cable at thy side.

Twist thou and twine! in light and gloom
   The spell is on thine hand;
The wind shall be thy changeful loom,
   Thy web the shifting sand.

Splendid stuff; but most of the anathema from Hawker and his kind was directed against legend rather than fact – if we are speaking of the deliberately induced wreck. The second crime, of not striving officiously to keep alive, is less easy to dismiss. In earlier times every sailor wrecked on these coasts knew he had two ordeals to survive: the sea and the men on shore, with little likelihood that the second would be kinder than the first. The real criminal here was Cornish ignorance of the law of dereliction. A very old and very bad statute, whose gist in a seventeenth-century formulation ran 'neither bird nor beast having escaped, for if anything had escaped alive, 'tis not to be adiudged Wreck', was taken as gospel in Cornwall long after it had lapsed elsewhere. It was to establish this definition – or invitation to murder – that first-instance survivors were sometimes knocked on the head and returned to the sea. The admiral of the *Association* fleet, Sir Cloudesley Shovell, is said to have reached land alive, and to have required a hasty re-drowning – though his own press-gangèd lower-deck men are quite as likely to have done that as the Scilly Islanders. But there are two much more recent and better-authenticated stories.

One concerns a Scillies wreck of the mid-nineteenth century. Two islanders on an abandoned ship were seen to throw a dog overboard and watch it drown. When reproached for their cruelty, they claimed the wreck would not have been 'dead' unless they had done it; and in his defence one of the men astonishingly quoted the relevant phrase from the original Plantagenet law. The second story is even more incredible. The steamer *Delaware* went aground during a huge storm in December 1871, near Bryher in the Scillies. Two survivors were seen to drift ashore on an uninhabited islet off Samson. Ten Bryher men – the old islanders were among the best handlers of small boats in rough seas in the world – managed, after superhuman efforts and with appalling risk to their own lives, to row a gig across to the islet. They were met with gratitude? Not at all, but by two terrified sailors with stones in their hands, convinced that their real fight for survival was still to come. Perhaps the most remarkable thing about this 1871 story is that the two men were not ignorant fo'c'sle hands, but respectively the first and third mates of the steamer.

The heroism (no isolated instance, and Bryher has a particularly fine record) of the rescuers that day is quite certainly more typical for all Cornwall, at any rate since 1800, than the stories of cold-blooded murder and deaf ears when 'near voices wildly cried'. The much more probable historical truth of the matter is summed up by a charming prayer – and conditional clause – composed in the Scillies in the late eighteenth century: 'We pray Thee, O Lord, not that wrecks should happen, but that if any wreck should happen, Thou wilt guide them into the Scilly Isles for the benefit of the inhabitants.' The girls of Tristan da Cunha had one very similar, if more frank: 'Please God send me a wreck, that I may marry.'

The third charge is of wreck-plundering, after the lives have been duly saved. Here, the only answer can be guilty. There are far too many eye-witness accounts of Cornish rapacity – indeed far more wreckers were themselves drowned looting than sailors murdered – to exculpate them. They would even board wrecks in the same seas that had caused their crews to abandon ship. When there was wreckers' weather ('A savage sea and a shattering wind, The cliffs before and the gale behind', according to an old couplet), whole villages, thousands of men and women with lanterns and axes and crowbars, with carts, wheelbarrows and sacks, would assemble like vultures; and follow a ship in trouble, for days if need be, along the coast. Even the largest vessels could be dismantled and stripped bare as a bone in twenty-four hours. The tin-miners were the most feared; no cliff, no storm, no night deterred them from getting to work once the ship had struck. Nor very often would they brook interference from magistrates or the military ... but the gentry themselves were not proof to the mania. Fine carriages as well as carts often flocked to the corpse. Even the excise men were suspect. Another story from the *Delaware* wreck of 1871 tells how the Chief Customs Officer of the Scillies prosecuted two men for looting – while his own backyard was full of drying bolts of silk. To add insult to corruption, for many months afterwards he was not seen smoking anything but fine Manilla cheroots.

The most famous of all such stories concerns the parson whose Sunday sermon was interrupted by the cry of 'Wreck!' outside. His congregation leapt to their feet as one man. 'One moment, my friends!' bellowed the reverend gentleman from the pulpit, as he struggled frantically to remove his surplice. 'Let's all start fair.'

Every respectable authority dismisses the story as apocryphal, mere foreign (i.e., English) prejudice. But I suspect it is one of those inventions that are truer than the truth; and perhaps I had better mention here that I have wreckers in my own ancestry, and even living to this day an 'Armada' uncle – dark-skinned, and sure proof in family legend that at least one foundered Spanish sailor ended in a Cornish bed rather than in (another foul lie from the wrong side of the Tamar) a Cornish pasty.

More seriously, all this ambivalence about personal and legal rights goes back to the ancient importance, in a rim-of-the-world economy, of benefit of wreck. This right was a major feature in many Cornish and Scillonian rent-rolls of the Middle Ages; and gave rise to ferocious disputes, sure sign of the profits involved, over boundaries and ownership of flotsam, jetsam, lagan (wreckage on the sea-bed) and the rest. I think today we may see it as a facet of the eternal struggle between the over- and the under-privileged. You cannot starve and ignore and despise a region to the permanent brink of famine and then expect it to wish the fattest ships in the world a safe journey past its shores; or to show fine scruples when some of the fat is washed up at its door. However much one respects the law, however deeply one is touched by the anguished tears of the ship-owners, I think one has to see a kind of profound equity, with the sea standing in the place of Robin Hood, in the phenomenon. I do not defend wrecking; but even less could I defend the gross social and economic selfishness of the ages and central governments when it flourished most strongly.

That these reefs and coasts remain hungry we still have evidence every year. But in the days of sail, and even of early steam, the statistics (if not the pollutions) were far worse. Between 1864 and 1869, the Lloyd's registers give a world loss of 10,000 sailing-ships. In 1856 alone 1,153 vessels were lost round the British coasts (and the figure for British ships lost abroad in that same year is only ten less). In *one* day of a great gale in 1859, 195 ships foundered; another 298 ships were lost in the terrible November of 1893. A great lack was of lighthouses. Before 1800 there were only four in all Cornwall, and two of them were coal-cresset beacons – the Lizard and St Agnes in the Scillies. The most-needed light in the world, the Bishop's Rock, was not finally in operation – after an extraordinary epic of Victorian engineering – until 1858. (On April 20th, 1874, in a gigantic storm, the largest waves were drowning the lantern a hundred feet above the normal sea and reflecting the light back into the keepers' eyes – the worst ordeal, the two men said, of their lives … and one believes them.)

Fortunately, if tragically, we know very well what it was like to be shipwrecked in the eighteenth and nineteenth centuries. Perhaps no form of human misery is so extensively recorded, and in every detail. No Royal Navy ship went down without a subsequent court martial of the senior survivor, and of course commercial ship-owners generally (but not always, for reasons I will explain in a moment) wanted full investigation from the Marine Courts. There was also the public fascination – shipwreck stories were once as popular as thrillers and sci-fi novels today – to say nothing of the need of the survivors, and of ghost-writers with an eye for easy money, to relate their adventures. I will quote just one splendid title of the kind from 1838: *Shipwreck of the Stirling Castle, containing a Faithful Narrative of the Dreadful Sufferings of the Crew, and the Cruel Murder of Captain Fraser by the Savages. Also, the Horrible Barbarity of the Cannibals inflicted upon the Captain's Widow, whose Unparalleled Sufferings are stated by herself, and corroborated by the Other Survivors.* I own a copy of this classic fragment of Australiana; and so also must that fine painter Sidney Nolan, who has immortalized poor naked Mrs Fraser in another way.

The most terrible experience must have been the catastrophe out of nowhere, at night or in fog. Again and again one reads the same story. There is a cry from forward of 'Breakers ahead!', then desperate commands to the helmsman, a wild scramble to get sails reset, to come up into the wind (which is why so many sailing ships in these circumstances first struck aft – missing stays and drifting impotently back). The masts sometimes helped if they crashed on impact and so formed a bridge of sorts, however precarious, to land. The more familiar prelude to disaster, storm, at least allowed crew and passengers to prepare themselves both psychologically and nautically for the worst.

Off mainland Cornwall the battle was sometimes prolonged for days when ships were caught inshore by a gale and fought desperately to beat out to windward. Some masters in this embayed situation struck all sail and topmasts to reduce windage and then anchored; but the old rope cables were not good and often parted. When the moment of truth came, all a captain could do was steer for beach or least precipitous cliff. Many times the ship struck and foundered as she came in or, most feared of all, turned beam on and capsized. After losing all her anchors, the frigate *Anson* did exactly this in 1807 at Loe Bar, and 120 men were drowned close to shore.

I mentioned earlier that navigational techniques were only too literally hit-or-miss. The situation improved when an accurate chronometer became available in 1772, but well into Vic-

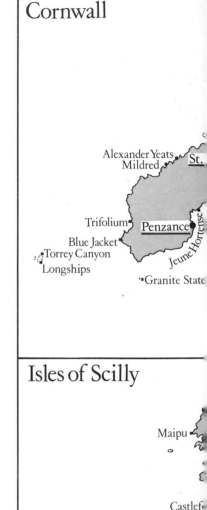

Cornwall

Alexander Yeats
Mildred
St.

Trifolium
Penzance
Blue Jacket
Torrey Canyon
Longships
Jeune Hortense

Granite State

Isles of Scilly

Maipu

Castlef

River Lune

torian times many ship-masters were far from skilled with the sextant. Then there was the condition of the ships themselves. Before Samuel Plimsoll's Merchant Shipping Act of 1876 they were often sent out criminally overladen, undermanned and rotten-timbered. Sailors had a name for them: coffin-ships. On a lee shore or in heavy seas that was only too often precisely what they were and also precisely what their astutely over-insured owners hoped they would be. This atrocious practice was rife, and Plimsoll deserves to be remembered for far more than his 'line'. The early steamships were not always much safer. Many were underpowered in relation to their size and became unmanageable in heavy seas. Their boilers also had a nasty habit of exploding when really put to the test.

Nor in the nineteenth century was the standard of seamen good. As with the wreckers, one can discover extenuating circumstances ... vile wages, peculating chandlers, brutal mates and masters. But the poor quality of the crews the average captain had to work with gave unnecessarily steep odds. One of the finest, because it is so plainly written, shipwreck accounts of the period is that of Thomas Cubbin. He was the experienced master of a sound merchantman, the *Serica*, but he ran into a hurricane off Mauritius in 1868. Long before he abandoned ship, his crew virtually mutinied; they tried to get at the liquor store, they refused to work the pumps. 'We're all equal now,' said one of them. Yet with a single exception (that old focus of gossip and sedition, the ship's cook) his was not a particularly bad crew; the impression one gets today is that they were far more demoralized than truly mutinous.

There is, from dry land, great poetry and drama about the shipwreck; but no sailor would let me suggest that the amusement of an audience is the heart of the matter. That heart lies, as it always has and always will, in the terror and despair, in the drowned, in the appalling suffering of the survived, the bravery of the rescuers. We should never forget that; and yet ... I should like to go now into the calmer, though deeper and darker, waters of why the spectacle of the shipwreck is so pleasing – why, in short, there is a kind of Cornish wrecker in every single one of us.

Our private attitude to communal disaster, the joint death of other people, could be regarded as unalloyedly humanitarian only by a supreme optimist; yet I should not like to call it, short of the pathological extreme, unhealthy. There is the Christian view: we feel pity for the victims. There is the Aristotelian: we feel purged, and go away better people. And so on, until we come down to the cynical: it is all a matter of *Schadenfreude*, and at least the population problem is relieved a little. But I'm not sure the most important reaction is not the instinctive: thank God this did not happen to me. In other words, we derive from the spectacle of calamity a sense of personal survival – as also, however tenuously, intimations of the metaphysical sea of hazard on which we all sail.

Perhaps one should not distinguish between train- and air-crashes, motorway pile-ups and all the other downstrokes that man the traveller is prone to; yet there is something rather special about the shipwreck, and I think not simply because it usually has a longer agony and a longer aftermath than death on land and in the air. The sea seems less greedy, for a start. Man's ability to endure in it against all the odds is a strange and incalculable thing. So many drowned men have crawled up a beach or been picked up in small boats weeks after they were consigned by all probability to Davy Jones's bottomless locker. But more important – at least for us spectators – than this intermittent show of mercy is surely the emotional symbolism.

This springs from two things: the nature of the sea and the nature of the ship. No other element has such accreted layers of significance for us, such complex archetypal meaning. The sea's moods and uses sex it. It is the great creatrix, feeder, womb and vagina, place of pleasure; the gentlest thing on earth, the most maternal; the most seductive whore, and handsomely the most faithless. It has the attributes of all women, and all men too. It can be subtle and noble, brave and energetic; and far crueller than the meanest, most sadistic human king who ever ruled. ('I believe in the Bible,' an old sailor once told Lord Fisher, 'because it don't mention no sea in Paradise.') I happen to live over the sea myself, I watch it every day, I hear it every night. I do not like it angry, but I've noticed that most urban and inland people adore it so. Storms and gales seem to awaken something joyous and excited in them: the thunder on the shingle, the spray and spume, the rut and rage.

No doubt this is partly a product of a life where the elements have largely receded out of daily notice; but I think it goes deeper, into a kind of Freudian double identification, in which the wrath of the sea is interpreted both as *super-ego* and as *id*. It is on the one hand a thing without restraint, a giant bull in a salt ring; on the other it is the great punisher of presumption, the patriarch who cuts that green stripling, man, down to size. It is strangely – or perhaps not so strangely, in these days of the universal oil-slick – as if we had committed a crime against the sea by ever leaving it in the first place; and as if we liked to be told (through convenient scapegoats, of course) that we merit retribution for our ambitious folly. In its rages we admire the total lack of reason and justice, the blindness to all but the laws of its own nature; and quite naturally, since similar feelings and desires lurk deep inside our own minds. A wrecking sea is part of what we all dream ourselves to be every night; and the ship becomes our own puny calculations, our repressions, our compromises, our kowtowings to convention, duty and a dozen other idols of

Trifolium

Wrecked at Whitesand Bay
(Sennen Cove), March 15th,
1914. This Gothenburg ship
was fifty miles off the Lizard
when her cargo shifted and
she was thrown on her beam.
Firing flares, she drifted in
among gale seas. Four men
were washed overboard close
to land, and three drowned.
The captain was hurled down
and killed on his own deck.
The crew went up in the
rigging, but the ship's motion
grew so wild that they could
not secure the rocket lines
from shore. The ship then
went abruptly to pieces.
Another man died. Five others
managed to get ashore, though
badly gashed by broken
wreckage.

the top-hamper we call civilization. A psychiatrist tells me that a morbid obsession with disaster is a common defence against depression; its enjoyment brings a vicarious sense of manic triumph over normal reality. So the shipwreck is not only what we are thankful will never happen to us; it is also what we secretly want to happen, and finally to ourselves.

The other great nexus of metaphors and feeling is the ship itself. No human invention, with all its associated crafts in building and handling, has an older history – or received more love. That is why we have sexed it without ambiguity, at least in the West; which in this context casts the sea, the domaine of Neptune, as raper, berserker, Bluebeard. Even our judgment of a ship's beauty has tended to be that of the male upon the female – that is, we put a greater value on outward line than on soul or utility, and nowhere more than with the last of the sailing-ships, that splendid and sharply individualized zenith of five thousand years of hard-earned knowledge and aesthetic instinct. The vocabulary of the aeroplane seduced us for a while; but I think it is interesting that we have come back to star- and space-*ships*. *Jet* will do for a transport shorthand; yet when man really reaches, across the vast seas of space, he still reaches in ships. Other words may function as well; no other has the poetries.

All this leads me to believe that there is, with the kind of shipwreck so finely illustrated here, a nobler constituent in our fascination … a genuine sadness. These photographs are of lost craft, but in both senses of the noun; they are failed hopes, ventures, destinies, but also shattered monuments to countless generations of anonymous shipwrights and sailmakers, as tragic in their way as the vanished masterpieces of great sculptors. The Gibsons' pictures are like stills, they freeze for eternity. But in the real moving film of time, they were taken at a very transient and final moment in each ship's life. Few lasted more than a month or two after the photographs were taken; some not a week. What we are seeing here is the condemned cell, the haunted calm of the days between sentence and execution.

Just as there are found objects, so are there agonized ones. The mist comes down on the drowned *Mildred*, her masts and ultimate set of sails rise from the appeased water like an epitaph, a cross of remembrance, a lovely assemblage of rope construct and canvas cut-out, pre-echoing Matisse and Naum Gabo … we have our monuments to the Unknown Soldier. Will anyone ever give us a more beautiful celebration of the Lost Ship?

Mildred

Struck under Gurnard's Head in thick fog at midnight, April 6th, 1912. She was carrying slag from Newport to London. When she began to pound broadside on, the captain and crew launched a boat and rowed along the cliffs to St Ives. The *Mildred*, Cornish built and owned, was launched in 1889.

The Gibsons

Other men have taken fine shipwreck photographs, but nowhere else in the world can one family have produced such a consistently high and poetic standard of work, or over such a long period.

The Gibsons have lived in the Scillies since at least the seventeenth century. John Gibson (1827–1920), the photographic pioneer of the family, first owned a camera in the very early 1860s. He had been at sea since boyhood, but he started taking portraits between voyages and thus antedates Julia Cameron by several years. She first used a camera in 1865; while by 1866 John had taught himself enough to quit the sea and set up as a professional. By then he had a son, Alexander (1857–1944), who must in more ways than one be counted the most remarkable Gibson. He became a working partner with his father in 1871, when he was still only fourteen. A self-made scholar with a bent for the archaeological, and something of an eccentric, he was not one to suffer opposition – a trait that was later to have tragic consequences.

Alexander (like all the Gibsons a fine photographer of many things besides shipwrecks) was a great arranger – his time-consuming perfectionism in this is a Scillies legend – of the human element in his pictures, as he was also a great retoucher of his plates. Yet this 'improving' is done with such charm, and often with such striking effect, that it lends his technical skills, his instinctive eye for angle, a very individual flavour. A typical plate by him is inherently dramatic; it says something more than the overt subject. The *Granite State* photograph on the cover demonstrates this exactly: the group, the woman looking through the telescope, are not natural – yet something is being told that no unstaged scene could express. When the second generation of Victorian photographers receives the interest we now devote to the first, Alexander must earn more attention; some of his portrait studies of the poor and aged are also of the very highest quality.

Alexander's younger brother Herbert (1861–1937) had a special fondness for shipwrecks and kept on with them long after Alexander had found more interest in other fields. The two brothers' styles were often very similar and a number of plates cannot now be ascribed with certainty.

Granite State

Struck on the Runnel Stone, three miles south-east of Land's End, November 4th, 1895. This fine Yankee windjammer was making for Swansea from Falmouth. A navigation error by the mate seems to have been the cause of disaster. She was hauled off by a tug, but had to be towed to the nearest sandy bay, Porthcurno. She settled rapidly, and when the cargo of wheat began to swell the crew took to boats. The *Granite Stone* was soon afterwards destroyed completely by a gale.

Alexander's son James, who is still alive, was taken into the business (whose main studio was by then in Penzance) in 1916. He had ideas of independence that did not please his highly independent father, and there was a time of dissension. Alexander even opened another studio on St Mary's in rivalry to his son. It did not succeed, and the old man retired to the mainland in great dudgeon. A settlement was worked out whereby James was to have all the shipwreck plates. They were more or less thrown, unpacked, at a carrier – but by some miracle arrived back in the Scillies unharmed. That could not be said for Alexander's other island plates, for in a fit of Lear-like rage he threw every single one he possessed down the shaft of a tin mine. Fortunately a number remained in the St Mary's studio. Alexander spent his last years in Oswestry. He is said to have photographed to the end, but his Shropshire work has not been traced.

The Gibson tradition is now carried on by James's son Frank, whose own evocative work must be familiar to anyone who has ever stayed on St Mary's. Prints of all the photographs in this book, and of many others we have not had space for, may be bought from him.

Bibliography

Richard Larn and Clive Carter, *Cornish Shipwrecks* (David and Charles, Newton Abbot, 3 vols, 1969–71).
Cyril Noall, *Cornish Lights and Shipwrecks* (Barton, Truro, 1968).
Juliet du Boulay, *Wrecks of the Isles of Scilly* (*The Mariner's Mirror*, 1959).
Scilly Museum, *Shipwrecks around the Isles of Scilly*.
John Vivian, *Tales of the Cornish Wreckers* (Tor Mark Press, Truro, 1969).
John Arlott, *Island Camera* (David and Charles, Newton Abbot, 1972).

Earl of Arran

Struck a rock in St Martin's Neck, then deliberately grounded on Nornour in the Scillies, July 16th, 1872. Built in Scotland in 1860 and a former Clyde excursioner, this paddle-steamer was by 1872 one of the two Penzance–Scilly packets. The captain allowed himself to be talked into using a short cut by one of his passengers, Stephen Woodcock – a pilot-boat sailor, though not himself a pilot. The 92 passengers, crew and cargo were saved, but the *Earl* was finished. Captain Deason had his certificate suspended for four months. A Stephen Woodcock rowed in the Bryher gig during the celebrated 1871 rescue of the mates of the *Delaware* mentioned in the Introduction; if it was the same man, he can hardly have been so popular in 1872 … especially when the other packet, the *Little Western*, was wrecked three months later. Again the captain was to blame – though on this occasion his demon was not a passenger, but brandy.

Rosa Tacchini (left)

Dragged on to Paper Ledges, just south of
Tresco, November 23rd, 1872. This Italian barque
had come to shelter inside the Scillies the previous
day, but the gale made her part anchor. Her masts
were cut away in an attempt to save her. Out of
Buenos Aires, her cargo was of hides, tallow and
wool; the port she never reached, Antwerp.
The original plate has been heavily retouched,
with figures added and others erased. Note the
decorative cabin aft; many Victorian masters
sailed with their wives and children.

Minnehaha (right)

Drove on to Peninnis Head (St Mary's, Scillies),
January 18th, 1874. She had taken fourteen
months bringing a cargo of guano from South
America to Falmouth, and was on her way to
discharge at Dublin. A north-west gale was
blowing when at 3 a.m. Captain Jones ordered a
course that might have saved the ship; but,
without his knowledge, the Channel pilot
countermanded it. The *Minnehaha* struck with all
sails set, and sank almost at once. The crew took
to the rigging. Captain Jones undressed, cried
'With God's help I will save all your lives!' and
leapt into the huge sea. He was never seen again.
The mate, more intelligently if less heroically,
waited in the rigging till daylight and then led
nine of the crew along ropes and yards until they
could leap ashore. Nine other men were drowned,
including the pilot, whose body was washed up
near Padstow two months later. This may well be
a very early plate by Alexander Gibson: both the
onlookers and the extensive retouching (the two
sails were added in the studio) are characteristic.
Among the most important customers for the
Gibsons in the early days were the survivors of
shipwreck. No old salt could be accused of
yarn-spinning with photographs like this to back
him.

River Lune (left)

Struck in fog and at night just south of Annet (Scillies), July 27th 1879 – the same day as the *Maipu*. The master later blamed a faulty chronometer, since he had believed himself fifteen miles to the west. The ship heeled and sunk aft in the first ten minutes. The crew took to their boats, but returned in daylight to collect their belongings. This barque was only eleven years old. She broke up soon afterwards.

Maipu (right)

Wrecked in Hell Bay on the north-west of Bryher, July 27th, 1879. There was fog, and the captain sensed he was in danger and started to wear ship; but she struck and began sinking by the bows. The wreck was sold to some Bryher men for £7, but it went to pieces three weeks later. Hell Bay is aptly named, and in a heavy sea without hope or mercy ... though a magnificent spectacle from land.

Castleford (left)

Ran ashore in thick fog on Crebawethan, among the Scillies' Western Rocks, June 8th, 1887. The principal cargo was 450 head of cattle, most of which were saved. The bemused creature in the foreground is on an islet more famous for its seals than its steers. Cattle-ship wrecks were popular with the islanders, since salvage money ran as high as £5 a head. Even burying the drowned carcasses was profitable. The islanders refused to inter those from the *Castleford* for less than thirty shillings each.

Bay of Panama (right)

Drove into cliffs at Nare Point near Falmouth, March 10th, 1891. One of the most famous and terrible of all Cornish wrecks. The *Bay of Panama*, an exceptionally fine ship, was off Cornwall carrying jute from Calcutta when she was caught in the blizzard of '91, a storm still remembered in the West. At 1.30 a.m. the ship was pooped – a huge wave swept her from end to end and smashed every boat. Soon after that, in blinding snow, she went headlong into the cliffs. Another monstrous wave swept nine people overboard, including the captain, his wife, and four apprentices. The mate got the crew up in the rigging, not without further loss, and at least six
continues over page

froze to death during the night. The boatswain went
mad and leapt into the sea. Seventeen of the original
crew of forty managed to survive until morning and
were brought ashore by breeches-buoy, as if fossilized
in ice, their limbs immovable. Though they were
well looked after at St Keverne, their agony was not
over. The horse-drawn omnibus taking them to
Falmouth the next day was caught in a snow-drift
and they had to finish their journey on foot – some
without shoes. As grim an ordeal as the shipwreck,
it was later said.

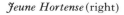

Jeune Hortense (right)

Stranded near St Michael's Mount, May 17th, 1888.
The foreground carriage is for the Penzance lifeboat.
This sturdy brigantine lived to sail another day.

Horsa (left)

Drove ashore in a cove of St Martin's (Scillies), April 4th, 1893. Homeward bound from New Zealand, she came too close inshore in a gale and missed stays. That same afternoon she was pulled off the rocks by the Scilly packet-steamer *Lyonesse*, the idea being to tow her round to St Mary's. But the ropes kept parting and eventually the captain tried to make his own way. Luckily he asked the packet to stand by, for at 1.30 a.m. on the 5th the *Horsa* rolled over and sank in deep water. The *Lyonesse* managed to save everyone. This misleadingly sound-looking full-rigger is therefore really in the last few hours of her life.

Alexander Yeats (right)

Struck in heavy seas under Gurnard's Head, September 26th, 1896. This large barque, out of Savannah with pitchpine, had had a week of trouble. She had been nearly wrecked at Milford on the 20th. On the 25th, in a rising south-west gale, her deck cargo shifted. Two lifeboats went out, but could do nothing to save the ship. The crew were rescued by breeches-buoy. Note the still suspended topmast.

Mohegan

Struck the Manacles, October 14th, 1898. One of the most dreaded of all reefs, the Manacles (from the Cornish 'maen eglos', rocks of the church, a reference to the landmark of St Keverne's tower) stand east of the Lizard promontory, in a perfect position to catch shipping on the way into Falmouth – and before Marconi 'Falmouth for orders' (as to final North European destination) was the commonest of all instructions to masters abroad. But the *Mohegan* was outward bound, and hers is one of the most mysterious of all Victorian sea-disasters. She was a luxury liner on only her second voyage, from Tilbury to New York. Somewhere off Plymouth a wrong course was given. A number of people on shore realized the ship was sailing full speed (13 knots) for catastrophe; a coastguard even fired a warning rocket, but it came too late. The great ship struck just as the passengers were sitting down to dinner. She sank in less than ten minutes, and 106 people were drowned, including the captain and every single deck officer, so we shall never know how the extraordinary mistake, in good visibility, was made. The captain's body was washed up headless in Caernarvon Bay three months later. Most of the dead were buried in a mass grave at St Keverne, where Alexander Gibson took this simple but eloquent plate.

Blue Jacket (left)

Stuck fast – and surely a classic example of the expression – on the Longships lighthouse rocks off Land's End, December 9th, 1898. This tramp was in ballast from Plymouth to Cardiff. The captain went below to his cabin – and his wife – at 9.30 p.m., leaving the mate on watch. He was woken near midnight by a tremendous crash, and came on deck to find his listing ship brilliantly illuminated by the lighthouse only a few yards away. Captain, wife and crew took to their boats and were picked up by the Sennen lifeboat. How the mate managed to play moth to this gigantic candle – the weather was poor, but provided at least two miles' visibility – has remained a mystery. The *Blue Jacket* sat perched in this ludicrous position for over a year.

Seine (right)

Ran ashore in Perran Bay (Perranporth), December 28th, 1900. This beautiful ship was a French 'bounty clipper' – so called because a government subsidy to French ship-owners allowed them to build for elegance rather than more mundane qualities. The crew got off in heavy seas. By dawn the next day she was dismasted and on her beam-ends, and broke up on the next flood-tide. Two weeks later the hulk of this celebrated barque was bought for only £42.

Voorspoed (left)

Ran ashore in a northerly gale
in Perran Bay, March 7th,
1901 – very near the *Seine*
wreck of the previous year.
The *Voorspoed* was carrying
general cargo (it included
a stuffed alligator) and
deserves a place in history as
one of the last wrecks to be
looted. The Dutch
captain said afterwards:
'I have been wrecked in
different parts of the globe,
even in the Fiji Islands, but
never among such savages as
those of Perranporth.' The
Voorspoed was evidently a
doomed ship, for although she
was refloated, on her next voyage
(to Newfoundland) she went
down with all hands.

Glenbervie (right and
Title page)

Struck on the Manacles and
went aground near Lowland
Point, December 1901. The
crew were saved in heavy seas
by the Coverack lifeboat. The
old wreckers must have
groaned in their uneasy graves
when they heard that this
cargo was officially salvaged,
since it contained over a
thousand cases and barrels of
spirits. There was also a valuable
consignment of grand pianos
on board, which were all
ruined. The *Glenbervie* was
launched in 1866; she was first
a tea-clipper, then had many
years in the Canada trade. She
normally made three trips a
year, between the thawing and
the freezing of the St
Lawrence, on this latter run.

Reginald (left)

Ran aground on the Gibsons' doorstep, the south-east coast of St Mary's, 1902. A reminder of the rare lighter side of being shipwrecked – she was a Plymouth trawler, and the crew brewed up while they waited for the next tide, which duly floated her off.

Noisel (right)

Driven ashore at Praa Sands in Mount's Bay, August 7th, 1905. Ships that failed to round the Lizard in southerly gales were trapped in Mount's Bay, or embayed ... many of them being unable to sail at all close to the wind. Their crews' only consolation was the presence of the many sandy beaches. Surf may drown, but granite cliffs do far more terrible things to the human body. The *Noisel* had been sailing from Cherbourg to Italy with a cargo of armour plate, but she met a heavy gale off Ushant and had to run for Plymouth when the cargo shifted and a list developed. Forced into Mount's Bay, the captain tried to anchor. The cable parted, and a second anchor dragged on the sandy bottom. Eventually the ship went broadside through the breakers and broke her back. Six of the crew leapt into the sea and the first realization on land of the wreck was an old lady's, who saw a black face peering through her window. It belonged to the ship's cook, a New York Negro. A line was got aboard and the rest of the crew brought off, though two had been drowned in the first attempt. The *Noisel*'s cargo of armour plate may still be seen after scouring seas.

Socoa (left)

Stranded near Cadgwith (Lizard), July 31st, 1906. Out of Bayonne, she was carrying cement from Stettin to San Francisco, where it was desperately needed following the great earthquake of earlier that year. After jettisoning 50,000 barrels, she managed to refloat. She was later renamed the *Thiers*, and was not broken up until 1927.

Suevic (right)

Struck on the Maenheere ('menhir') Rock off the Lizard Head, March 17th, 1907. This 12,500-ton liner was coming in from Australia with 456 passengers and crew (and one stowaway) when a combination of poor visibility and poor navigation brought her to grief. There followed the most successful rescue in the history of the lifeboat service – not a soul was lost. The ship was so badly damaged that she was eventually blown in half. The aft section was towed to Southampton and a new bow built. The *Suevic* was a troopship during the First World War, and then a whaling factory ship ... and she died honourably. Her Norwegian crew scuttled her in 1942 to save her from falling into German hands.

Susan Elizabeth (above)

Driven ashore at Porthminster Beach (St Ives), October 17th, 1907. A gale blew this collier's sails out off the Mumbles. Less than three months later the *Lizzie R. Wilce* and the *Mary Barrow* also had to beach here.

Lizzie R. Wilce and *Mary Barrow* (right)

Both driven ashore on Porthminster Beach, January 7th, 1908. The *Lizzie R. Wilce* (nearer the camera) missed stays and had to beach. The lifeboat had hardly gone back to its house before the maroons were fired again, as the *Mary Barrow* (both ships were carrying coal from Swansea) came in almost alongside. The latter was refloated and worked as a coaster until 1938. The *Lizzie* was launched in 1874, a clipper-built schooner especially designed for the pineapple trade. She never sailed again, and ended her life as a coal-hulk.

A Scilly Gig (left)

At work after the grounding of the liner *Minnehaha* on Scilly Rock, April 18th, 1910. This ship, out of New York for Tilbury, had been going slowly because of fog. Once again the Bryher gigs went to the rescue and helped land all the passengers. Also on board were 230 steers, some of whom can be seen swimming beside the gig. The liner had to be lightened, and brand-new American motor-cars, pianos, harmoniums, tobacco barrels, and many other things were jettisoned ... to the profound delight of the islanders.

The main purpose of the unique six-oared Scillonian gig was to row island pilots out to ships. It was a question of first come, first hired, so these gigs were renowned for their speed and strong oarsmen; as also for their coxswains' superb handling, even in mountainous seas.

Pindos (right)

Stranded at Chynhalls Point (Lizard), February 10th, 1912. The *Pindos* was British built and British owned for the first six years of her life, but in 1896 she was sold to a Hamburg shipping company. In 1911 she had carried bricks to South America, and then brought nitrates back to Falmouth. She was in tow for Hamburg when she was caught in a strong south-easter on leaving the Carrick Roads. The tug could not hold her and at 9 p.m. she was carried broadside on the reefs. The German crew were saved during the night. More gales soon broke this large ship to pieces.

Saluto (left)

Dragged ashore at Perranuthnoe
(Mount's Bay), December 8th, 191[
This old ship, launched in 1867, ha
sprung a leak beyond the Scillies on
her way to Barbados. Her sand ball
turned to mud and choked the
pumps. On her limping way back to
Falmouth she was forced into
Mount's Bay. The crew were taken
off by lifeboat and landed at Newly
among cheering crowds and to the
accompaniment of the Salvation
Army Band.

Hansy (right)

Wrecked in Housel Bay near the
Lizard Point, November 13th, 191[
Sailing from Sweden to Melbourne
with timber and pig-iron, she misse
stays while trying to come about in
gale. The crew were brought ashore
by breeches-buoy. Two days later a
salvage party boarded – to find a pa
of goats lying happily in a seaman's
bunk. Local fishermen did a thrivir
trade in timber for weeks afterward
and the iron pigs are fished up for
ballast to this day. The Scottish-bu
Hansy (formerly *Aberfoyle*) had had
an unhappy history. In 1890 the bu
of the crew jumped ship in Austral
after a bad voyage out – only to be
returned on board following a
fortnight in jail. Jail must have beer
more agreeable, for eight men jump
ship again at the next port of call.
In 1896 a steamer found the *Aberfo*
drifting helplessly off Tasmania. T
captain had been swept overboard,
the first mate had committed suicic
by leaping into the sea and the rest
had given up hope. Similar stories
low morale – and often of insane
bitterness between officers and crev
are manifold.

Gunvor (left)

Struck on Black Head (Lizard) during fog, April 6th, 1912. Another large ship, and, like the *Pindos*, bringing nitrates from South America. She lodged so close that the Norwegian crew escaped with the greatest of ease down the rope ladder still seen hanging from the bowsprit in the photograph.

Tripolitania (right)

Driven ashore at Loe Bar (Mount's Bay), December, 1912. She was sailing from Genoa to Barry in ballast, but ran into a hurricane-force storm in the Bay of Biscay. Her high hull and the 100 m.p.h. winds soon put her in grave trouble. In Mount's Bay the captain deliberately ran ashore at full speed through high surf. The Italian crew threw a rope over the bows, slid down it and swam through the waves. All but one made land. Attempts to salvage her lasted for nearly a year, but eventually she broke up. The *Tripolitania* had formerly been British and by a strange coincidence her last British master, Captain Beckerleg, lived at Marazion, only a few miles from where his old ship met her end.

Cromdale (left)

Grounded in dense fog at Bass Point (Lizard), May 23rd, 1913 – only ten days and half a mile from where the *Queen Margaret* came to grief. This ship, carrying nitrates, was wrecked just before ten o'clock in the evening and had to be abandoned almost immediately. The crew got safely off. A week later a gale broke the ship for good.

Longships (above)

Stranded and broke her back on the Seven Stones, December 22nd, 1939. The Seven Stones lie between Land's End and the Scillies. The *Longships* was sailing from Belfast to Plymouth and strangely ended her days almost within sight of the lighthouse after which she was named. The reef's most famous victim is of course the *Torrey Canyon*.

Torrey Canyon

Gashed open on Pollard Rock, one of the Seven Stones, March 18th, 1967. The dreaded Seven Stones lie fifteen miles west of Land's End and 7 miles east of the Scillies. The second largest vessel ever lost at sea, the *Torrey Canyon* was carrying just short of 120,000 tons of crude oil. She was travelling at 17 knots, in broad daylight and a calm sea, with near-perfect visibility; and struck at 8.45 a.m. The subsequent appalling pollution – the oil could be smelt far into Devon – and the final decision to bomb the wreck is too well known to need retelling. The tragedy began with a landfall error more characteristic of the eighteenth than the twentieth century. The Italian captain, *en route* from the Gulf to Milford Haven, had meant to pass west of the Scillies, but found himself east when his radar first picked up the islands to the north. He decided to use that passage rather than follow his much safer original plan. That no one on the bridge seemed aware of the reef, with three lighthouses visible, to say nothing of the Seven Stones lightship itself, is so implausible that one wonders why sailors ever gave up their belief in the siren.